Knowing God by His Names

DICK PURNELL

HARVEST HOUSE PUBLISHERS

EUGENE, OREGON

Cover by Terry Dugan Design, Bloomington, Minnesota

KNOWING GOD BY HIS NAMES
Copyright © 2005 by Dick Purnell
Published by Harvest House Publishers
Eugene, Oregon 97402
www.harvesthousepublishers.com

ISBN-13: 978-0-7369-1510-6
ISBN-10: 0-7369-1510-9

Printed in the United States of America

08 09 10 11 12 / BP-CF / 10 9 8

And I will do whatever you ask in my name, so that the Son may bring glory to the Father. You may ask me for anything in my name, and I will do it (John 14:13-14).

To my wife, Paula

*You are a good and perfect gift from
the Father of the Heavenly Lights (James 1:17).
May your light shine brilliantly for Him all the days of your life.*

Contents

Knowing and Loving
the One True God

❧

Do you want to know what God is really like? Does your heart
yearn to love Him more?

Love is built on knowledge—the more you understand His
true character and ways, the more you will love Him.

Because God is way beyond human beings, the only way to
know what God is really like is to know what He reveals about
Himself. That is where the Bible comes in. The Bible is God's
letter revealing Himself and His ways.

Have you wondered how to get something—anything—
from the Bible? It seems so complicated, so big, so tough. So to
know the true God seems like an impossibility.

I thought that way until…

One Sunday evening a man who was leading worship in my
church service stopped the music and said, "The name of God
we are singing about comes from Psalm 18. By understanding
His name, you will have greater insight into who He really is. In
fact, there are many more names for the Lord in the Psalms."

That caught my attention. I wanted to know God intimately,
so I started a search for God's names revealed in the Bible. It

took me six years to study thoroughly every verse in the Old and New Testaments.

The wealth and richness of the titles God uses for Himself overwhelmed me.

The more I found, the more I wanted to know. And in the process my heart was being drawn closer to the Lord. Every spare minute I studied to discover additional information about my heavenly Father and how I could love Him more deeply.

It's key to remember that a name to the people in biblical times meant something entirely different from what it does to us today. In our culture a name rarely reflects hopes for a child's future or character. It is usually a reflection of ethnicity, culture, or parental preference.

A name in the Bible is rich with purpose and meaning. The giving of a name or the changing of a name was auspicious. A name encompassed the hopes and dreams for the person or offered a prophetic glance into the character of the one being named. A change of name signaled a new relationship or a new phase of life or new destiny. For example, the Lord gave Jacob the name Israel when he was a middle-aged man (Genesis 32:27-28). God was not trying to reidentify him. He desired to change his inner character from Jacob ("deceiver") to Israel ("one who interacts with God").

God revealed each of His names in a specific situation where one of His people had a special need. The name that was revealed related directly to the aspect of His character that would provide the solution to the problem that person was facing.

For example, when little David faced huge Goliath, he proclaimed, "You come against me with sword and spear and javelin, but I come against you in the name of the LORD Almighty, the God of the armies of Israel, whom you have defied" (1 Samuel 17:45). The name "LORD Almighty" reveals He is all-powerful, and "God of the armies of Israel" means He is the Supreme General leading His army into battle. How could Goliath possibly win against those odds?

Our great Lord has over 200 names! God has so many names because no one name could tell you everything there is to know about His transcendent character. Each name puts the spotlight on one of His marvelous attributes. The more you know about His names, the more you will understand His complex character—and the more you will love Him. As you grow in your knowledge and love of God, your faith will grow as you place greater confidence in the Sovereign Lord.

Try this experiment to develop intimacy with the true, revealed God. It won't take you six years—just 31 days. For one month, dig for the glorious riches found in God's names. You will find yourself on an adventure into the supernatural ways of the Most High God.

Get ready for a life-transforming experience. At the end of a month you may be so excited about your growing relationship with our Lord that you will want to continue to enhance your faith. In the back of this book is a list of 207 names of God. Find one of them that interests you and search the Bible to discover all that it reveals about the Almighty God.

Although this book is small in size, what you learn as you study the names of God will continue to affect you for the rest of your life. You will become passionate to "love the Lord your God with all your heart and with all your soul and with all your mind" (Matthew 22:37).

"Those who know your name will trust in you, for you, LORD, have never forsaken those who seek you" (Psalm 9:10). Notice how the Lord's actions are tied to His names and, then, how His names reflect His attributes. When you know that He always acts consistently with His character, your faith will not be weakened by difficult circumstances or troubling times. The King of Kings will give you strength and peace.

"'Because he loves me,' says the LORD, 'I will rescue him; I will protect him, for he acknowledges my name'" (Psalm 91:14). Your prayer life will be transformed. Right now you may close your prayers with a casual "in Jesus' name, Amen." But you will learn that praying in Jesus' name means to pray according to His attributes and promises. You will come to appreciate that your faith-filled prayers relate to things that are in the heart of God and based on the character of His Beloved Son.

"And I will do whatever you ask in my name, so that the Son may bring glory to the Father. You may ask me for anything in my name, and I will do it" (John 14:13-14). When you have a need, or when you want to praise Him, address God using the name that deals with that situation.

Praying this way will challenge your thinking about who the Lord really is, and it will deepen your relationship with Him. When you become fearful and insecure, look to the King of Kings. In an atmosphere of turmoil and stress, depend on the Prince of Peace.

When you are hurt, come to Jehovah-Rophe (the Lord Who Heals). If you have sinned, find forgiveness from the Lamb of God. As you enter dark times, follow the Light of the World.

These names do not refer to many gods: there is only one God—the triune God—but three distinct persons: God the Father, God the Son, God the Spirit. They are equal in nature and attributes, but they are distinct in personality and function. Therefore, some of the names are used interchangeably for all three, such as God or LORD. But others refer to a specific person of the Godhead, such as heavenly Father, Savior, or Holy Spirit.

According to the Bible, the goal of your life is to glorify God through faith in Him and obedience to His Word. As you increase your understanding of the triune God and deepen your love for Him, He will reveal more of who He is and His ways to you. Your heart will sing praise to our wonderful King. The psalmist put it this way: "But let all who take refuge in you be glad; let them ever sing for joy. Spread your protection over them, that those who love your name may rejoice in you" (Psalm 5:11).

My Prayer

Dear Heavenly Father,

I want to know You as intimately as a human being is able. In my busy life filled with pressures and hectic activities, it is often difficult for me to think about You. My relationship with You frequently fluctuates between genuine love and cold neglect.

I want to love You more consistently and experience Your presence daily. Please strengthen my faith in You. Give me the discipline to daily spend time in the Bible and prayer for the next 31 days—and for the rest of my life.

King of Glory, open my mind to Your spectacular majesty. My precious Savior, draw my heart closer to You with Your infinite love and marvelous grace. Spirit of Truth, guide me to understand more clearly the complexity of the triune God.

May this experiment change my life permanently!

In the name of the Lord Jesus Christ. Amen!

Signed _____

Date _____

My Covenant with God

I promise the Lord Jesus Christ that I will do this Experiment in Knowing God by His Names. During the next 31 days I will do the following:

1. Spend 20 to 30 minutes each day in Bible study, prayer, and writing out my thoughts and plans.

2. Ask at least one other Christian to pray daily for me that I will be consistent in doing this experiment (that person may want to do the experiment along with me so we can share together what we are learning).

3. Attend a church each week where the people enthusiastically worship the King of Kings and Lord of Lords.

Signed _____

Date _____

Guidelines to Knowing God Better by His Names

Preparation for Each Day

1. Equipment. Obtain a translation of the Bible that you enjoy reading. If you want to use the same translation used in this book, look at the *New International Version* (NIV). Get a pen to record in this book. Journal your thoughts, answers to prayers, and plans.

2. Time. Pick the time of day when your heart will be the most receptive to meeting with God. Try to make a habit of meeting with the Lord at a specific half-hour each day.

3. Place. Find a particular spot where you can clear your mind of distractions and focus your full attention on God's Word. Suggestions: bedroom, office, school library, living room, outdoors.

Read (10–20 Minutes)

1. Pray earnestly before you begin. Ask the Spirit of Truth to teach you what He desires you to learn.

2. Read the entire passage that is the selection for the day.

3. Read it again, looking for God's names that are revealed. There may be several. Notice what kind of response He wants from you.

4. Make written notes on the following:

> A and B—Study the passage thoroughly to answer the questions. Focus your attention on the attributes and actions of our great God. The more you know about Him, the more you will be able to trust Him to work in and through your life.

> C—Write out your personal responses and specifically apply the lessons you have learned.

5. Choose a verse from the passage you just read that is especially meaningful to you. Copy it onto a card and read it several times during the day. Think about its meaning and impact on your life. Memorize it when you have free mental time; for example, when you are getting ready in the morning, while you are standing in line, during lunch, taking a coffee break, waiting for class to begin, or walking somewhere.

Need (5 Minutes)

1. Choose your most pressing personal need of the day.

2. Write down your request. The more specific you are, the more specific the answer will be.

3. Faithfully pray each day for the provision of the Sovereign LORD. Trust Him for big things.

4. When the heavenly Father meets your need, record the date and how He did it. Periodically review the wonderful

provisions of the Son of God and thank Him often for His faithfulness. This will greatly increase your faith.

5. At the end of the month, review all the answers to your prayers. Rejoice in the Living God's goodness to you. Keep praying for the requests that still need answers.

Deed (5 Minutes)

1. Pray for the Great Shepherd's guidance to help another person during the day. Try to apply the particular passage you have just studied.

2. Take the initiative to express Messiah's wonderful love to someone. Be a servant. Behind every face there is a drama going on. Tap into at least one person's drama each day. Serve that person and speak about what you are learning.

3. As you help a needy person, tell him or her about your faith in Christ. Here are some suggestions for helping someone:

    a. Provide a meal.

    b. Take care of someone's children for an evening.

    c. Help a friend study for a school test.

    d. Do yard work with a neighbor.

    e. Write an encouraging letter.

    f. Start a Bible study.

    g. Teach someone a sports activity or a mechanical skill.

    h. Assist in moving household possessions.

    i. Take someone out to lunch and listen to the needs expressed.

    j. Fix something for a neighbor.

    k. Show interest in another's interests.

    l. Give an honest compliment.

  m. Pray with a friend about a need.

    n. Contribute money to a missions cause.

    o. Visit someone in the hospital or at a retirement home.

4. Later, record the details of how the Holy Spirit used you this day. This will increase your confidence to reach out to others. Thank the Lord Jesus for expressing His love and compassion to others through you.

Application

1. Write down your thoughts about how you can put into practice specific instructions and ideas found in the passage.

2. Devise a plan to implement your ideas.

Last Thing in the Evening

1. **Read**—Look at the passage again, searching for additional ideas about Jehovah's character.

2. **Need**—Pray again for your concerns. Thank the Lord that He will answer in His way and in His time. Expect the Spirit of the Living God to strengthen you in your walk with Him.

3. **Deed**—Record how God guided you to accomplish something for Him.

4. **Application**—Review what you learned today. Look for further biblical insight to help you apply the passage to your life.

Doing This Experiment with Others

Ask a friend or a group of friends to do the experiment with you. Read in the back of this book "How to Lead a Group of People to Know God Better by His Names" for practical suggestions.

Pray frequently for one another that you will learn more about the God of Glory and how to live for Him. Encourage one another to be disciplined and faithful in completing the experiment. Share what you are learning and how the heavenly Father is working in your lives.

The Experiment:

31 Days Focusing on Knowing God by His Names

Those who know your name
will trust in you,
for you, LORD, have never forsaken
those who seek you.

PSALM 9:10

DAY
1

God (Elohim)

Genesis 1:1-31

Key Verse:

In the beginning God created the heavens and the earth (Genesis 1:1).

Today's Focus:

Before there was anything, there was God. The English name "God" in the Old Testament is usually a translation of the Hebrew name "Elohim," meaning "omnipotent power." It refers to the Lord's absolute dominion over the whole universe. It is used 3,393 times from Genesis to Malachi. God's power goes beyond any force in the whole universe.

Read: Pray to understand the magnitude of God's power and how He can change your life.

  A. Study the creation events. Describe what God created on each day of creation.

     1.

     2.

     3.

4.

5.

6.

B. For what purposes did God create humans?

C. Because God is the Creator of the universe and all that it contains, He is my Maker. I am so grateful to Him for:

Need: Praise God for the beautiful world He made.

My greatest need today is:

Today _____ (date) God answered my need by:

Deed: Pray for courage and boldness to serve Him.

God, do Your powerful work through me to:

*A*pplication:

Make a list of all the attributes God displayed when He created the universe and everything in it. (For example, the stars and vastness of space show that God has infinite wisdom.)

DAY
2

God Almighty (El-Shaddai)

GENESIS 17:1-27

Key Verse:

When Abram was ninety-nine years old, the LORD appeared to him and said, "I am God Almighty; walk before me and be blameless" (Genesis 17:1).

Today's Focus:

God Almighty is a translation of the Hebrew name "El-Shaddai." El is the root of Elohim and refers to His mighty power. The word *shaddai* means breast and refers to God's nourishing and sustaining us. Thus, El-Shaddai is all-powerful to meet our needs and fulfill His promises, according to His will and His timetable.

Read: Pray for greater faith in God Almighty.

A. When Abraham was 75 years old, God promised to give him descendants who would become a great nation (Genesis 12:1-9). But at the age of 99, he still did not have a son. What did God Almighty promise this old man?

B. How did Abraham show that he believed Him?

C. When God Almighty promises me through His Word to do "impossible" things, I will:

Need: Thank God Almighty that He always keeps His promises.

My greatest need today is:

God Almighty showed Himself sufficient to answer my need today _____ (date) by:

Deed: Pray that you will experience El-Shaddai's power in your life.

God Almighty, do Your will through me today by:

*A*pplication:

What is one significant promise God Almighty has made in His Word that applies to your situation? Have you done your part by obeying? How has He fulfilled His promise?

DAY 3

LORD (Jehovah)

EXODUS 3:1-22

Key Verse:

God said to Moses, "I AM WHO I AM. This is what you are to say to the Israelites: 'I AM has sent me to you'" (Exodus 3:14).

Today's Focus:

"I AM" is actually the Hebrew word *Yahweh*. The ancient Hebrews changed the pronunciation of the letters to Jehovah. This name has been translated into the English word LORD with the last three letters in small capitals. It appears over 6,000 times in the Old Testament and is the most frequently used name. LORD refers to His eternal nature and supremacy (sovereignty) over all heaven and earth. He is always present with His people.

Read: Pray for a deeper knowledge of the LORD's character.

A. The Hebrew people had been enslaved in Egypt for hundreds of years. God chose Moses, an 80-year-old shepherd, to lead about 500,000 Hebrews out of slavery. In the process He revealed His name "I AM" (Jehovah), which assures His people that He is in control of all things. What characteristics does the LORD reveal about Himself in this passage?

B. What was Moses' reaction to the LORD's command?

C. When the LORD asks me to do something difficult, I will:

Need: Pray for freedom from any sinful attitude or action that has you in bondage.

My greatest need today is:

The LORD answered my prayer today _____ (date). Here's how:

Deed: Thank Jehovah that He is with you right now—and always.

Eternal LORD, lead me to:

*A*pplication:

Jehovah is written as LORD to distinguish it from another Hebrew name, Adonai, which is also translated Lord but rendered in uppercase L and lowercase "ord" (see Day 9). In the New Testament the Greek word *kurios* is translated as Lord. Jesus claimed to be "I AM" (Jehovah) in John 8:48-59. Study how the religious leaders reacted to Christ's astonishing statement.

DAY
4

LORD Who Heals
(Jehovah-Rophe)

EXODUS 15:1-27

Key Verses:

There the LORD made a decree and a law for them, and there he tested them. He said, "If you listen carefully to the voice of the LORD your God and do what is right in his eyes, if you pay attention to his commands and keep all his decrees, I will not bring on you any of the diseases I brought on the Egyptians, for I am the LORD, who heals you" (Exodus 15:25-26).

Today's Focus:

The English phrase "the LORD, who heals you" is a translation of the Hebrew name for God "Jehovah-Rophe." Sometimes you may be tempted to think the LORD doesn't want to help you, or that your trouble is too small for Him to think about. When those thoughts come, remember that God has the power to heal the big and small hurts of those who obey Him.

Read: Pray for God's power to heal hurts in your life.

A. The Israelites left Egypt and slavery, but as they came to the Red Sea, the Egyptian warriors closed in to destroy them. The LORD miraculously delivered His people. What did the people thank Him for?

B. Three days later they faced another dilemma. How did they react?

C. When I am confronted with a difficult dilemma, I will:

Need: Thank Jehovah-Rophe for helping you.

My greatest need today is:

Today _____ (date) the LORD Who Heals answered my prayer. Here's how:

Deed: Pray for opportunities to share about God's healing power with others who are experiencing pain in their lives.

Jehovah-Rophe, please guide me to give encouragement and comfort to others in this way:

*A*pplication:

What is the significance of the name Jehovah-Rophe (the LORD Who Heals)? How has He brought healing into your life? Recall what He's done for you in the past and thank Him for His power and faithfulness. Make a list of the hurtful things you are now dealing with. Ask Him to heal them.

DAY 5

Rock

DEUTERONOMY 32:1-47

Key Verse:

He is the Rock, his works are perfect, and all his ways are just. A faithful God who does no wrong, upright and just is he (Deuteronomy 32:4).

Today's Focus:

God is a refuge and a source of security. When times get tough, you can depend on the Rock. You can confidently trust Him because He does not change, and He keeps His promises throughout all generations.

Read: Pray to take to heart God's words.

A. After wandering in the wilderness for 40 years, the Israelites were getting ready to enter the Promised Land. Moses reminded them of their relationship with God. What are the characteristics of the Rock, and what does He do for His servants?

B. How did the Rock treat those who turned away from Him?

C. My response to God, my Rock, is:

Need: Pray for confidence in God's ways.

My greatest need today is:

God, my Rock, answered my prayer today _____ (date) in this way:

Deed: Pray for courage to proclaim the name of the Lord.

God, my Rock, guide me to:

*A*pplication:

Our God is the Rock, a refuge from troubles and a source of strength. Name the things that are bringing stress and pressure into your life. How can the Rock shelter you?

DAY
6

God Who Sees (El Roi)

GENESIS 16:1-16

Key Verse:

She gave this name to the LORD who spoke to her. "You are the God who sees me," for she said, "I have now seen the One who sees me" (Genesis 16:13).

Today's Focus:

God sees you no matter where you are. He not only knows all about you, but He loves you. He sees and cares. When you are confused, needy, or weary, call upon Him. Trust El Roi to guide you through even the most difficult circumstances.

Read: Praise El Roi that He sees and cares for you.

A. Hagar was a servant, a lowly status in the household of Abram and Sarai. What problems did she face, and why did she run away?

B. What was it about El Roi that assured Hagar she could trust Him?

C. When I feel like I just want to run away from my problems, I will look to the God who sees me because:

Need: Pray for the LORD's comfort and guidance:

My greatest need today is:

El Roi answered my prayer today _____ (date) like this:

Deed: Ask for insight to see the problems of others.

O El Roi, other people I know or will meet need to understand that you see and care for them. Guide me to help them to:

*A*pplication:

Read about some other people in the Bible who saw the Lord and understood His caring for them. Look at Job's response after God revealed how He sees and cares (Job 42). Read Paul's testimony of seeing the light of Jesus on the road to Damascus (Acts 26).

DAY 7

Judge of the Earth

PSALM 94:1-23

Key Verses:

> For the LORD will not reject his people; he will never for-
> sake his inheritance. Judgment will again be founded on
> righteousness, and all the upright in heart will follow it
> (Psalm 94:14-15).

Today's Focus:

God's judgment is fair, equitable, and based on truth. He is
the final Judge who will expose evil and lift up His righteous servants. As His child, you need not fear His judgment if you're
living according to His ways.

Read: Pray for a clean heart and courage to obey Him in all
circumstances.

A. A judge has the authority to make significant decisions in
a court of law. What attributes does the Judge of the Earth
possess that qualify Him to make the final judgment on
every person?

B. Compare how He treats two kinds of people:

Righteous people	Wicked people

C. I humble myself before the Judge because:

Need: Thank the Lord that His love supports you.

My greatest need today is:

Today _____ (date) the Judge of the Earth answered my prayer in this way:

Deed: Pray for His consolation in times of anxiety.

O Judge of the Earth, open up the way for me to:

Application:

Have you been wronged by someone? Give your thoughts and feelings to the righteous Judge who will someday right all wrongs. Trust Him to deal with the situation in His own way. Study Romans 12.

DAY
8

God of Israel

1 Kings 8:1-30

Key Verse:

O LORD, God of Israel, there is no God like you in heaven above or on earth below—you who keep your covenant of love with your servants who continue wholeheartedly in your way (1 Kings 8:23).

Today's Focus:

The name "God of Israel" appears 195 times and represents the Lord's sovereignty over the nation and His people. Because He is the Supreme Ruler, He is able to keep His promises. Thus, His people can trust Him in the midst of all circumstances.

Read: Pray to walk before God with your whole heart.

A. Since the time of Moses, God's presence with His people was symbolized by the ark (a portable, golden chest containing the tablets of the Law). Because the people were now settled in the land, Solomon built a magnificent temple, which symbolized God's presence and where

people could worship the Lord. At the dedication ceremony, what did he say was so great about the God of Israel?

B. What did he ask God to do for His people?

C. I dedicate my life to the God of Israel and ask Him to:

Need: Pray for perseverance in keeping His commandments.
My greatest need today is:

Today _____ (date) the God of Israel answered my
prayer. Here's how:

Deed: Thank the LORD that He hears our prayers.
God of Israel, I praise Your name and ask:

*A*pplication:

Is there something you would like to commit totally
to the God of Israel (yourself, a family member,
home, etc.)? Put together and perform a dedication
ceremony to the Lord. Ask Him to fill that person or
thing with His presence.

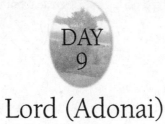

DAY
9

Lord (Adonai)

ISAIAH 6:1-13

Key Verse:

Then I heard the voice of the Lord saying, "Whom shall I send? And who will go for us?" And I said, "Here am I. Send me!" (Isaiah 6:8).

Today's Focus:

In the Old Testament, the name "Adonai" is translated into English as "Lord" and appears 412 times. Adonai means master or owner and refers to God's right to possess and rule His creation. Even so, He gives human beings the choice to obey or disobey Him. We bear the consequences of our choices. When the voice of the Lord calls, choose to obey.

Read: Pray for a glimpse of His majesty.

    A. Describe in your own words what Isaiah saw when he looked at the Lord (Adonai).

B. Why do you think Isaiah responded the way he did?

C. When Adonai asks, "Whom shall I send? And who will go for us (the triune God)?" my response is:

Need: Pray for forgiveness for the times you failed to obey the Lord's call.

My greatest need today is:

Adonai answered my prayer today _____ (date) in this manner:

Deed: Pray for obedience to Adonai's commandments.

Lord, to whom are You sending me today?
Give me the opportunity to:

*A*pplication:

Reread today's passage and notice the usage of the words LORD (Jehovah) and Lord (Adonai). Now read Psalm 110:1, Matthew 22:41-46, and Acts 2:32-36. Who is the Lord (Adonai)? Who is LORD (Jehovah)? What causes you to believe that?

DAY 10

Prince of Peace

ISAIAH 9:1-7

ꞁꞁ

Key Verses:

> *And he will be called Wonderful Counselor, Mighty God, Everlasting Father, Prince of Peace. Of the increase of his government and peace there will be no end* (Isaiah 9:6-7).

Today's Focus:

When you're worried, frightened, stressed, unsure, or doubtful, call on the Prince of Peace. The peace He offers will calm your soul, ease your mind, and rest your heart.

Read: Pray for His peace in the midst of storms you are facing.

A. For hundreds of years Israel had disobeyed God by doing wicked and evil things. Even though the Lord punished them severely, He promised them hope through the coming child (Christ). List all His names given in this passage and their meanings.

B. Just before He went to the cross, Christ offered hope and peace of mind to His followers in John 14:1-4, 26-27, and 16:33. How was the Lord living up to His name given in Isaiah?

C. My response to the Prince of Peace is:

Need: Pray for peace of mind.

My greatest need today is:

The Prince of Peace met my need today _____ (date) in this manner:

Deed: Pray for troubled people to experience His peace.

I believe God will show me the way to:

*A*pplication:

What things are troubling you and causing you to worry? Describe how you can receive God's peace in those areas.

DAY 11

Holy One

Key Verses:

> *When you pass through the waters, I will be with you; and when you pass through the rivers, they will not sweep over you. When you walk through the fire, you will not be burned; the flames will not set you ablaze. For I am the Lord, your God, the Holy One of Israel, your Savior* (Isaiah 43:2-3).

Today's Focus:

God is absolutely pure and perfect. He does not, and cannot, lie. What He says, He means. You can count on that. There is no deceit or guile in Him. The Lord's holiness reveals our sin and need for forgiveness. He hates all sin, but loves and raises up His people who humble themselves before Him.

Read: Thank the Holy One that He is with you—always.

A. Because of the terrible wickedness of the people, the southern two tribes comprising the nation of Judah (also called Jacob or Israel after the fall of the northern ten tribes of Israel) was destroyed by Babylon in 587 BC.

However, the Holy One still was committed to His people. What did He promise them?

B. What facts about the Holy One show that He is the unique God who is far above all other gods?

C. Because the Holy One loves me, and I am precious in His sight, I:

Need: Thank the LORD that He created you for His glory.

My greatest need today is:

The Holy Spirit answered my prayer today _____ (date) in this way:

Deed: Pray for courage to proclaim His praise.

O Holy One, help me tell a needy person of Your restoring power to:

Application:

When you face difficulties and you walk through "fire," how do you know for sure that the Holy One can be trusted to guide you through the struggles?

DAY
12

Living God

JEREMIAH 10:1-25

Key Verse:

> *The LORD is the true God; he is the living God, the eternal King. When he is angry, the earth trembles; the nations cannot endure his wrath* (Jeremiah 10:10).

Today's Focus:

God is alive! All of the things that clamor for your time and attention will cease to exist one day. But not God. It often looks like evil is in control of our world. But do not fear. The Living God still lives, and He will conquer all unrighteousness. He is truly worthy of your worship and allegiance.

Read: Pray for a receptive heart.

A. The Israelites were tempted to worship the gods of the surrounding powerful nations. Compare their idols with the Living God.

Idols	Living God

B. What other names for the Living God are found in this passage? What does each tell you about Him?

C. I reject all idols in my life and choose to serve the Living God because:

Need: Thank God He is alive and lives in you.

My greatest need today is:

Today _____ (date) the Living God answered my prayer in this way:

Deed: Pray that the Lord will reveal any idols that may be in your life.

Living God, lead me to:

*A*pplication:

An idol does not have to be something made of gold or wood. An idol in your life is anything that lessens your allegiance to the Living God. What are the idols in your life? What hinders you from wholehearted devotion to the Lord? Pray that the Lord will reveal to you any idols that may be in your life. Confess them, and return to total commitment to the Living God.

DAY 13

Shepherd (Jehovah-Rohi)

Ezekiel 34:1-31

Key Verses:

For this is what the Sovereign LORD says: I myself will search for my sheep and look after them. As a shepherd looks after his scattered flock when he is with them, so will I look after my sheep (Ezekiel 34:11-12).

Today's Focus:

God is a loving, attentive, compassionate Shepherd to you. You can trust Him to care for you. Because you are one of His sheep, He will rescue and guide you as well as provide for your needs.

Read: Pray for the Shepherd's care and guidance.

A. Israel and Judah paid a high price for their evil ways and their wicked leaders (shepherds). But the faithful were still God's people. What does the Shepherd do for His sheep? Contrast this with the false, evil shepherds of Israel.

God our Shepherd	False shepherds

B. Describe the Shepherd's attributes.

C. I will follow Jehovah-Rohi, my Shepherd, because:

Need: Praise the Lord for His showers of blessing in your life.
My greatest need today is:

The Shepherd took care of my need today _____ (date)
by:

Deed: Thank God your Shepherd for everything He has done in your life.
Lord, lead me to shepherd Your flock. I am available to:

*A*pplication:

How has Jehovah-Rohi shown you that He is your Shepherd? Write down all the times He has guided you and protected you. Be specific, and thank Him for each one.

DAY 14

God of Heaven

DANIEL 2:1-49

✤

Key Verses:

Then Daniel praised the God of heaven and said: "Praise be to the name of God for ever and ever; wisdom and power are his" (Daniel 2:19-20).

Today's Focus:

No matter how powerful and important a human being may be, he or she is nothing compared to the majestic God of Heaven. He rules heaven and has everything in the universe under His control—past, present, and future. His wisdom and power provide the answers we need for today, tomorrow, and every day.

Read: Pray for God to do "impossible" things in your life.

A. Daniel was probably a teenager when he was deported by the Babylonians after they had captured Jerusalem. He quickly rose to prominence because of his trust in the God of Heaven. What did Daniel believe about Him?

B. How can you be confident that the God of Heaven has the future in His hands?

C. I pray that the God of Heaven will do the following through me:

Need: Pray for God's leadership in every aspect of your life. My greatest need today is:

The God of Heaven met my need today _____ (date) in this way:

Deed: Pray for courage to motivate others to trust the God of Heaven.

God of Heaven, help me to:

Application:

Read Nehemiah 1–2 to see how the God of Heaven worked in a totally different situation. What are some "impossible" things you are facing? Ask the God of Heaven for the wisdom and power for specific solutions. Write down additional verses in the Bible that refer to God's sovereignty and majesty.

DAY
15

Most High God

DANIEL 4:1-37

Key Verses:

> *It is my pleasure to tell you about the miraculous signs and wonders that the Most High God has performed for me. How great are his signs, how mighty his wonders! His kingdom is an eternal kingdom; his dominion endures from generation to generation* (Daniel 4:2-3).

Today's Focus:

The Most High God displays great signs and wonders! He is far above all other earthly powers. You can worship Him for He is majestic. And you can experience His greatness in your life—if you will believe Him.

Read: Pray to experience the Most High God's greatness.

A. King Nebuchadnezzar of Babylon had conquered all the countries of the known world. Yet, one day he met his match. Here is his testimony of how he came to believe in the Most High God. Summarize it in your own words.

B. What adjectives describe the Most High God?

C. Here is the testimony of my faith in the Most High God:

Need: Pray for genuine humility to live for Him.

My greatest need today is:

The Most High God met my need today _____ (date) by:

Deed: Pray for the opportunity to share your testimony.

I pray the Most High God will:

*A*pplication:

Write out your testimony of how you came to put your faith in the Most High God. Share it with someone today.

DAY 16

LORD Almighty (Jehovah-Sabaoth)

ZECHARIAH 8:1-23

Key Verses:

> *This is what the LORD Almighty says: "Many peoples and inhabitants of many cities will yet come, and the inhabitants of one city will go to another and say, 'Let us go at once to entreat the LORD and seek the LORD Almighty. I myself am going'"* (Zechariah 8:20-21).

Today's Focus:

The name LORD Almighty appears 249 times in the Old Testament. It signifies that He reigns with power, compassion, and righteous judgment. He is vitally concerned for His people and their welfare.

Read: Pray to seek the LORD Almighty and entreat Him to work mightily in your life.

A. After the destruction of Judah and the scattering of its people throughout the world, Zechariah predicted their return to Zion (Palestine). What is the LORD Almighty like? What did He promise to do for His people?

B. What did He command His people to do?

C. I will obey the LORD Almighty because:

Need: Pray to follow the LORD Almighty with your whole heart.

My greatest need today is:

The LORD Almighty met my need today _____ (date) by:

Deed: Pray for others to worship the Lord with you.

LORD Almighty, give me Your strength to:

Application:

Other translations of the Bible render Jehovah-Sabaoth as "LORD of Hosts." The word *Sabaoth* means "hosts" (a large number of beings organized for battle). He is the powerful leader of the army of heaven. He punishes the rebellious and raises up the faithful. Read 2 Samuel 7 to discover what He said to King David. Where have you seen His transforming power at work in your own life?

DAY 17

Savior

LUKE 2:1-40

Key Verses:

But the angel said to them, "Do not be afraid. I bring you good news of great joy that will be for all the people. Today in the town of David a Savior has been born to you; he is Christ the Lord" (Luke 2:10-11).

Today's Focus:

Finally, in God's time and way He fulfilled His promise to give to a sinful world a precious gift—a Savior. The provision for mankind's sin came in a baby boy who would eventually grow up to save us from the consequences of our sins (eternal destruction). The good news on that first Christmas (and for the world today) is that Jesus is the Savior we desperately need.

Read: Thank God that He sent us the Savior.

A. What were the reactions of people to the birth of Jesus? What did they believe about Him?

Shepherds	Mary	Simeon	Anna

B. The results of the Savior's sacrifice are given in Titus 3:3-8. What did He do for those who put their trust in Him?

C. I am thankful for Jesus, my Savior, because:

Need: Pray for a greater passion to glorify God.

My greatest need today is:

The Savior answered my prayer today _____ (date) in this manner:

Deed: Pray for open doors to share with others the joy of your salvation.

Dear Savior, spread the message of Your offer of salvation through me to:

*A*pplication:

The death of the Savior on the cross makes salvation available to all. His resurrection proves He was God and breaks the stranglehold of sin and death. But only certain people actually receive salvation. What does a person have to do to receive it?

DAY 18

The Word

JOHN 1:1-18

Key Verses:

In the beginning was the Word, and the Word was with God, and the Word was God. He was with God in the beginning (John 1:1-2).

Today's Focus:

God is a spirit. Because we human beings are sinful, we cannot understand the spiritual realm. So to communicate with us directly, God became a man. He is called the Word of God because He came with a message. Jesus Christ is God, and transforms those who believe in Him.

Read: Praise God for coming to Earth to show us Himself.

A. Jesus Christ is the Word of God. List all the characteristics that He displayed.

B. He created the world. But how did people (those He created) respond to Him? What does He do for those who believe in Him?

C. I believe the following things about the Word of God:

Need: Praise God for His amazing grace toward you.

My greatest need today is:

The Word of God met my needs today (date) in this way.

Deed: Pray for God's grace and truth to fill your life.

Jesus, people need to know You and believe Your message. Strengthen me today to be Your witness to share with someone. I would like to talk with:

*A*pplication:

Jesus is coequal with God the Father and God the Spirit. He is eternal, holy, Creator of all, and divine. Study more about His deity in Mark 8:27-38; 2 Corinthians 5:1-21, and Colossians 1:15-23. How are you changed when you believe in Christ?

DAY 19

Christ

JOHN 1:19-51

%%

Key Verse:

The first thing Andrew did was to find his brother Simon and tell him, "We have found the Messiah" (that is, the Christ) (John 1:41).

Today's Focus:

Christ is God in the flesh who came to Earth. The name "Christ" appears 532 times in the New Testament and means "anointed one." It is a title of deity signifying His official designation as Messiah—God's long-promised provision for the world's need for a right relationship with Him.

Read: Thank Christ for coming to save us.

A. What did each of these people believe about the Christ?

John	Andrew	Philip	Nathanael

B. What other names did these people call Christ? How does each one expand your understanding of Him?

C. My response to Christ is:

Need: Pray for faithfulness in following Christ.

My greatest need today is:

Christ answered my prayer today _____ (date). Here's how:

Deed: Pray for courage to tell others about Christ.

I want to be like Andrew and bring _____ (person's name) to Christ. Help me to:

*A*pplication:

To further your understanding of Christ, read what Peter said about Him in Matthew 16:13-28. Why do you think Peter believed that? What was Christ's response?

DAY 20

Messiah

JOHN 4:1-42

ᘒ

Key Verses:

> *The woman said, "I know that Messiah" (called Christ)*
> *"is coming. When he comes, he will explain everything to*
> *us." Then Jesus declared, "I who speak to you am he"*
> *(John 4:25-26).*

Today's Focus:

Before the foundation of the world, God had a plan to reconcile sinful humanity to Himself. The coming of Messiah was the fulfillment of that plan. The Hebrew word for *messiah* and the Greek word for *Christ* both mean "the anointed."

Read: Praise God for His fulfilled promises in sending the Messiah.

   A. For hundreds of years the Jews had been looking for God's promised Messiah. What convinced the Samaritan woman that Jesus was the long-awaited fulfillment of that promise? And what was her response to Him?

B. What did the disciples learn in this passage?

C. I believe Christ is the Messiah because:

Need: Pray for strength to accomplish God's work.

My greatest need today is:

The Messiah answered my prayer today _____ (date) in this manner.

Deed: Pray that others will believe in Jesus because of your testimony.

Messiah, send me to:

Application:

Make a list of the people you would like to see come to believe in the Messiah. Start praying earnestly and consistently for them. Trust Him for a harvest of souls.

DAY 21

Light of the World

JOHN 9:1-41

Key Verse:

> *While I am in the world, I am the light of the world* (John
> 9:5).

Today's Focus:

In a society lost in the darkness of immorality, injustice, and sin, Christ's light shines brilliantly. Only the Light of the World can enlighten the darkened hearts of people and lead them to eternal truth.

Read: Thank Christ for lighting up your life.

A. How did Jesus show that He is the Light of the World?

B. How did the blind man react to receiving physical eyesight? Spiritual eyesight?

C. Here is how Jesus brought His light into my dark heart:

Need: Pray for healing and spiritual sight.

My greatest need for today is:

The Light of the World met my need today _____(date) by:

Deed: Pray for boldness to talk about Jesus.

Lord, I want to work Your works while it is light. Use me to:

Application:

List the things that prevent you from being a bold witness for Christ. Next to each one write how you can overcome that obstacle through Christ's strength. Read a book on how you can become a better witness for Him.

DAY 22

Father

JOHN 17:1-26

Key Verses:

Righteous Father, though the world does not know you, I know you, and they know that you have sent me. I have made you known to them, and will continue to make you known in order that the love you have for me may be in them and that I myself may be in them (John 17:25-26).

Today's Focus:

God the Father is the heavenly Father—perfect, loving, compassionate. His family consists of Christ, His Son, and those who put their faith in Him. He desires for each person to believe in Him and thus become His child—forever.

Read: Pray for a deeper understanding of God's love for you.

A. The people of Christ's day had no concept of the fatherhood of God. When Jesus talked about His intimate oneness with God the Father, it was startling and revolutionary.

Just before He went to the cross, Christ poured out His heart in prayer. Describe His relationship with the Father.

B. What did Jesus ask the Father to do for those who believed Him?

C. I know that I am in God the Father's family because:

Need: Pray for greater understanding of your relationship with the Father.

My greatest need today is:

My heavenly Father met my need today _____ (date) by:

Deed: Pray for oneness with other believers.

Father, show me how to be in harmony with:

*A*pplication:

Eternal life is to know God the Father (John 17:3). In the Bible the word *know* means both intellectual knowledge and experiential understanding. What can you do to know Him better?

DAY 23

Son

Key Verse:

The Son is the radiance of God's glory and the exact representation of his being, sustaining all things by his powerful word. After he had provided purification for sins, he sat down at the right hand of the Majesty in heaven (Hebrews 1:3).

Today's Focus:

What is God really like? He is perfectly represented in His Son, Jesus Christ. The triune God is one God but three distinct persons (God the Father, God the Son, and God the Spirit). Understanding the Son will enhance your knowledge of the Father and the Spirit. They are all equal.

Read: Pray for clearer understanding of the Trinity.

A. The deity of Jesus Christ is emphasized in His name, Son. He is eternally distinct in personality from the Father and the Holy Spirit. Yet, He possesses the same nature and attributes. Describe the uniqueness of the Son.

B. How is He different from angels?

C. I believe that Jesus is God the Son because:

Need: Thank the Father for sending His Son to Earth.

My greatest need today is:

The Son answered my prayer today _____ (date) in this way:

Deed: Pray for opportunities to explain to someone that Jesus is God.

I want the Son to:

*A*pplication:

Do you have questions about the Trinity? Write them out and try to find the answers through other passages in the Bible, such as those in the book of John. Look in a Bible encyclopedia and theology books.

DAY 24

Son of Man

MATTHEW 24:1-51

Key Verse:

So you also must be ready, because the Son of Man will come at an hour when you do not expect him (Matthew 24:44).

Today's Focus:

Christ is called the Son of Man 89 times in the New Testament. It designates Him as the highest representative of mankind to God. How wonderful that He bridges the gap between sinful people and the Holy One! And He is coming back to bring His followers to the Father.

Read: Thank Christ that He is your representative to the heavenly Father.

A. What makes the Son of Man different from everyone else?

B. How is the Son of Man described?

C. Since the Son of Man is coming back soon, I want to live
in this way:

Need: Pray to follow Him faithfully.

My greatest need today is:

The Son of Man met my need today _____ (date) by:

Deed: Pray for others to learn of Christ.

Son of Man, I ask You to:

*A*pplication:

The title Son of Man was Christ's favorite descrip-
tion of Himself. No one else called Christ by that
name. Look in the rest of Matthew for the other
times He called Himself the Son of Man. What did
He say about His purposes for coming to earth?

DAY 25

Jesus

ACTS 2:14-47

Key Verse:

Therefore let all Israel be assured of this: God has made this Jesus, whom you crucified, both Lord and Christ (Acts 2:36).

Today's Focus:

Jesus was one of us, but He was also divine. He was fully God and fully man, the God-Man. His earthly life, death, and resurrection have profoundly affected mankind's history. For those who choose to follow Him, He changes their lives.

Read: Thank God Jesus came to Earth.

A. List and explain the characteristics of Jesus that Peter proclaimed in his Pentecost sermon.

B. How were the lives of new believers changed?

C. This is what I believe about Jesus:

Need: Thank God for raising Jesus.

My greatest need today is:

Jesus answered my prayer today _____ (date) in this manner:

Deed: Pray for a sharing attitude.

Jesus, give me Your power to:

*A*pplication:

The resurrection of Jesus shows that He is God and that He can change our lives. What are the evidences that Jesus arose from the grave? How has He affected your life?

DAY 26

Lord Jesus Christ

2 THESSALONIANS 1:1–2:17

Key Verses:

May our Lord Jesus Christ himself and God our Father, who loved us and by his grace gave us eternal encouragement and good hope, encourage your hearts and strengthen you in every good deed and word (2 Thessalonians 2:16-17).

Today's Focus:

Christ is referred to as Lord more than 550 times. The title "Lord" signifies Jesus' authority to rule over all creation, in your heart, and in your life.

Read: Pray to trust and obey Him in all circumstances.

A. How will Jesus show He is Lord over all?

B. What will happen to believers? To unbelievers?

C. Jesus Christ is my Lord! Therefore, I will:

Need: Pray that your faith and love will increase.

My greatest need today is:

The Lord Jesus Christ answered my prayer today _____ (date) by:

Deed: Pray to glorify the name of the Lord Jesus.

Dear Lord Jesus Christ, work in my life to:

*A*pplication:

The passage states that you are "loved by the Lord" (2:13). How has Christ shown you that He loves you?

DAY 27

Spirit of God

1 CORINTHIANS 2:1-16

Key Verses:

> *For who among men knows the thoughts of a man except the man's spirit within him? In the same way no one knows the thoughts of God except the Spirit of God. We have not received the spirit of the world but the Spirit who is from God, that we may understand what God has freely given us* (1 Corinthians 2:11-12).

Today's Focus:

There are over 400 passages in the Bible referring to the Spirit, the third Person of the Trinity (coequal with God the Father and God the Son). One of the many names for Him is the Spirit of God because He reveals the deep things about the Father and the Son to believers.

Read: Thank the Spirit of God for revealing God to you.

A. The Spirit of God is the source of everything you need for your Christian experience. Describe what He does for those who believe in Christ.

B. Why doesn't a non-Christian understand what the Spirit of God reveals? Who does understand?

C. I want to know more about God the Father. So I ask the Spirit of God to:

Need: Ask the Spirit of God to teach you more about the Lord.

My greatest need today is:

The Spirit of God answered my prayer today _____ (date) in this way:

Deed: Pray for the Spirit to teach you how to live by God's truth and wisdom.

O Spirit of God, help me to communicate what God is like to:

Application:

Look in a Bible concordance for all the references to the Spirit. Write down all His attributes that you can find. Which of the Spirit's functions have you experienced in your life? Trust Him to continue working in and through you.

DAY 28

Counselor

JOHN 14:15-31

Key Verses:

> *All this I have spoken while still with you. But the Counselor, the Holy Spirit, whom the Father will send in my name, will teach you all things and will remind you of everything I have said to you* (John 14:25-26).

Today's Focus:

The Lord Jesus left the Earth, but gave us the Spirit as our Counselor to teach us all that He wants us to know. He is the divine comforter of believers. If you love Christ, you will show that love by obeying what the Spirit reveals. He lives in you— you are never without the presence of God.

Read: Thank God the Father and Christ for giving you the Holy Spirit, your Counselor.

A. When Jesus told the disciples He was leaving, they were upset, fearful, and confused. What would the Counselor do for them?

B. What adjectives would you use to describe the Counselor?

C. I need the Counselor to help me in so many areas. I am
going to trust Him to:

Need: Pray to obey Christ in everything.

My greatest need today is:

The Counselor (the Holy Spirit) solved my need today
_____ (date) by:

Deed: Thank the Counselor that He lives in you.

Holy Spirit, my Counselor, use me to share God's truth with:

*A*pplication:

Read John 15:26-27, Acts 9:31, Romans 8:26-27,
and 2 Corinthians 1:3-4 to learn about what the
Spirit can do in your life as you trust Him. Tell Him
you are willing to do whatever He directs you to do.

DAY 29

Spirit of Truth

JOHN 16:1-16

Key Verses:

> *I have much more to say to you, more than you can now bear. But when he, the Spirit of truth, comes, he will guide you into all truth. He will not speak on his own; he will speak only what he hears, and he will tell you what is yet to come* (John 16:12-13).

Today's Focus:

Learning the truth and living by it is one of the most important issues of life. To believe and live a falsehood leads to disillusionment and negative consequences. The Spirit of Truth will lead you to know God's truth and will empower you to live by it.

Read: Praise God that the Spirit of Truth reveals what is right.

A. List all the things that the Spirit of Truth (Who is also called the Counselor) will do when He comes.

B. What did Jesus predict would happen to the disciples after He left?

C. I want the Spirit of Truth to work in my life in the following areas:

Need: Thank the Spirit of Truth that He guides you into God's truth.

My greatest need today is:

The Spirit of Truth met my need today _____ (date) by:

Deed: Thank the Spirit of Truth that He gives strength and encouragement to you.

Spirit of Truth, give me the words to say to a friend who needs to know the right things to believe about Christ. This is what I would like You to do:

Application:

Look at the other references to the Spirit of Truth in John 14:17 and 15:26, and 1 John 4:6. What are the functions of the Spirit of Truth in the world and in your personal life? Because there is no falsehood or deceitfulness in Him, you can put your faith in God's guiding you correctly. Make a list of the questions you have about God and ask Him to answer them as you continue to study His Word.

DAY 30

Lamb

REVELATION 5:1-14

❧

Key Verse:

*Worthy is the Lamb, who was slain, to receive power and
wealth and wisdom and strength and honor and glory
and praise!* (Revelation 5:12).

Today's Focus:

The Lamb of God took away the sins of the world. His sacrifice is our salvation. Without Him we are all doomed to eternal
destruction. He went to the extreme for us. Thus, He is worthy
of our unending praise and worship.

Read: Worship the Lamb.

    A. Why do all the elders, angels, and creatures worship the
Lamb?

B. Why is He worthy to open the scroll?

C. I worship the Lamb because:

Need: Thank Christ that He has promised His followers that they will be with Him in heaven someday.

My greatest need today is:

The Lamb met my need today _____ (date) in this manner:

Deed: Pray for courage to tell others about the Lamb.

O Lamb of God, I ask You to:

*A*pplication:

Compose your own song or poem of praise to the Lamb. Write a prayer that expresses your love for the Lamb of God. Read and pray it often.

DAY 31

King of Kings and Lord of Lords

REVELATION 19:1-21

Key Verses:

Out of his mouth comes a sharp sword with which to strike down the nations. "He will rule them with an iron scepter." He treads the winepress of the fury of the wrath of God Almighty. On his robe and on his thigh he has this name written: KING OF KINGS AND LORD OF LORDS (Revelation 19:15-16).

Today's Focus:

At the end of human history, when time has been completed, Jesus will reign supreme. Amen, hallelujah!

Read: Praise the Lord for who He is and what He has done.

    A. How does Jesus show that He is King of Kings and Lord of Lords? Describe Him.

B. What other names for Him appear in this passage? What does each one reveal about His character?

C. My response to the King of Kings and Lord of Lords is:

Need: Thank God He has invited you to the wedding supper of the Lamb.

My greatest need today is:

The King of Kings and Lord of Lords met my need today _____ (date) in this manner:

Deed: Pray for others to believe in Jesus, the mighty conqueror of the nations.

I am at Your command, O King of Kings and Lord of Lords, to:

*A*pplication:

Today is the last day of this experiment. Spend some extra time reviewing the names of God. Praise Him for all you have learned and experienced.

How to Expand
Your Knowledge of God
Through His Names

Congratulations! You have completed the experiment in developing a deeper intimacy with the LORD (Jehovah). After a full month of delving into the character of the Living God, you have probably realized that there is so much more to learn. The Lord Jesus Christ wants you to know Him in all of His fullness. What a fantastic invitation!

To walk with the LORD Almighty is the greatest adventure. It is worth the effort to discipline yourself to spend time reflecting on His other names. The Father invites you to feast upon His Word and to drink enthusiastically of the Living Water.

The following pages contain one of the most complete lists of the names of God you will find. However, it probably does not contain all of them. As I search the Scriptures, I continue to find additional ones. If you come across names I have missed, please write to me and tell me what they are. My address is in the back of this book.

But how do you study His names further? Using this list of God's names, follow the suggested study method below. Ask the

Spirit of God to instruct you in the path you should follow. Keep praying that your Bible study will result in greater godliness, deeper trust, and stronger faith.

Here is a simple plan to learn more about God and His fascinating names. Each one will reveal significant truths about the Lord's incredibly complex and fascinating character.

A. Facts to Discover

1. Choose one name at a time from the list of God's names that you wish to study.

2. Look for that particular name of God in a concordance representing the Bible translation you are using. Write out each verse that contains it. Study the most significant passages to glean new information.

3. Find the meaning of the name in a Bible dictionary or commentary.

4. Fill in the Chart of God's Names following the list. Follow the example given in the exhibit. For future reference, be sure to include in parentheses the verses where you find specific information. Each passage you choose will not necessarily have information for each category. But list everything you do find.

   a. Name—Name of God you want to study

   b. Passage—Significant verses in which the name is found as well as surrounding verses that explain it

   c. Characteristics—Attributes and actions of God that give you insight into His character

   d. Promises—Notice three types:

(1) Unconditional—God will do it no matter how people respond to Him.

(2) Conditional—God will do it only if the person or group of people obey Him.

(3) Warning—God will bring negative consequences if the person or group of people disobey Him.

e. Commands—Instructions the Bible gives you to obey

f. Response—Reaction of the people in the passage to God or His messenger

B. Things to Understand

1. Study the chapters and passages that come before and after the verse in order to get a complete picture of the meaning of the passage.

2. Look for statements that God makes about Himself. What insight do they give you into His mind and heart?

3. Observe the statements that people make about the Lord. Are they correct or incorrect?

4. Notice the other names of God in the passage. What additional information do they give you about His character?

5. Biblical authors may use the name in a variety of ways. How does that help you grasp the complexity of the title?

6. Investigate words related to the name. For example, if you are studying the King of Glory, study the words *king,*

sovereign, ruler, glorious, and *holy.* Related words will often open up additional understanding about God.

7. How does understanding the meaning of the name help you to: worship, praise, glorify, obey, and serve God?

C. Actions to Take

1. As you are studying, periodically pause to worship and praise God.

2. Compose a song or poem using the name.

3. When you pray, communicate your love and appreciation to God. Think about your requests and needs. Address the Lord using His names that emphasize those attributes that relate to your situation. For example, if you feel weak, pray using the name LORD God Almighty, Who gives security and strength to meet your need. If you need to make an important decision, seek the guidance of your Shepherd.

4. Incorporate the biblical truths you learn into your life. Focus on how they will affect your relationship with the Lord, yourself, family, friends, roommates, and others.

5. Teach the names of God to others. Start a small Bible study or lead a Sunday school class. Utilize the suggestions given in the section of this book, "How to Lead a Group of People to Know God Better by His Names."

6. Memorize favorite passages.

7. Meditate on significant thoughts about God. Let your mind and spirit dwell upon the complex beauty of our heavenly Father.

List of God's Names

Name	Key Passage	Characteristics
Advocate*	1 John 2:1	Helper, divine lawyer who pleads our case
Almighty (Shaddai)	Joel 1:15	Sovereign, All-powerful
Alpha and the Omega	Revelation 22:13	Beginning and end of all
Amen	Revelation 3:14	God's final seal of His promises
Ancient of Days	Daniel 7:9	Judge of the whole world
Angel of the LORD	Zechariah 12:8	Old Testament appearance of Christ
Anointed One	Daniel 9:25	Messiah, Ruler
Author of Life	Acts 3:15	Creator, Founder of life

*The word "Advocate" (*Paracletos* in Greek) appears in 1 John 2:1 (New American Standard Version), but is translated "One who speaks to" in the New International Version.

Name	Key Passage	Characteristics
Beginning and the End	Revelation 22:13	Before all and beyond all
Branch	Zechariah 6:12	Divine origin, descendant of David
Branch of the LORD	Isaiah 4:2	Beautiful life from God
Bread of Life	John 6:35	Satisfies our hunger for life and eternity
Breath of the Almighty	Job 33:4	Spirit of God, giving life, understanding
Chief Shepherd	1 Peter 5:4	Foremost of all leaders
Chosen One	Luke 23:35	Special to God, anointed
Christ	Matthew 16:16	Messiah, title of deity
Christ of God	Luke 9:20	Messiah from heaven
Commander of the LORD's Army	Joshua 5:15	Leads His people in battle
Cornerstone	1 Peter 2:6	Most important stone in God's building
Counselor	John 14:26	Comforter, encourager
Creator	Ecclesiastes 12:1	Maker of all
Creator of Heaven and Earth*	Genesis 14:19	Designer, Builder, Originator

* Translated as "possessor of heaven and earth" in the New American Standard Version.

Name	Key Passage	Characteristics
Deity	Colossians 2:9	Divine, God Himself
Deliverer	Romans 11:26	Rescuer, compassionate
Defender	Proverbs 23:11	Protector, fights for His people
Eternal God (El Olam)	Genesis 21:33	Forever Lord, infinite
Everlasting Father	Isaiah 9:6	Eternal relationship with His children
Faithful and True	Revelation 19:11	Trustworthy, righteous
Father	Galatians 4:6	God adopts us into His family, new relationship
Father of Compassion	2 Corinthians 1:3	Kind, sensitive
Father of the Heavenly Lights	James 1:17	Giver of perfect gifts
Fear of Isaac	Genesis 31:42	God that Isaac revered
First and the Last	Revelation 1:17	Beginning and end of all things
Glory	Psalm 106:20	Perfection, splendor

Name	Key Passage	Characteristics
Glory of Israel	1 Samuel 15:29	Supreme eminence of the nation
God	Hebrews 1:8	Christ is God
God (Elohim)	Genesis 1:1	All powerful, Creator
God Almighty (El-Shaddai)	Genesis 17:1	All powerful, keeps promises
God and Father of Our Lord Jesus Christ	Romans 15:6	First Person of Trinity, unique relationship with Christ, His Son
God Most High (El Elyon)	Genesis 14:18	Incomparable God, above all
God of Abraham	Genesis 31:42	Abraham's Lord
God of Daniel	Daniel 6:26	God that Daniel served
God of Earth	Genesis 24:3	Ruler of everything
God of Glory	Psalm 29:3	Magnificent, spectacular
God of gods	Psalm 136:2	Only true God, above all
God of Heaven	Nehemiah 1:4	Sovereign, commands heavenly beings

Name	Key Passage	Characteristics
God of Hope	Romans 15:13	Our security, provider
God of Isaac	Genesis 28:13	Isaac's Lord
God of Israel (Elohe-Israel)	Jeremiah 45:2	Leader of His people
God of Jacob	Micah 4:2	Lord of Israel, faithful
God of Jerusalem	Ezra 7:19	Ruler of the city
God of Jeshurun	Deuteronomy 33:26	Lord of Israel
God of Our Fathers	Ezra 7:27	Faithful, kind, unchanging
God of Peace	1 Thessalonians 5:23	Gives stability and victory
God of Retribution	Jeremiah 51:56	Punishes evildoers
God of the Armies of Israel	1 Samuel 17:45	Omnipotent, leads His people
God of the Hebrews	Exodus 5:3	Sovereign LORD of the people of Israel
God of Truth	Isaiah 65:16	Righteous, accurate
God of Your Fathers	Joshua 18:3	The one your ancestors worshiped
God Our Savior	1 Timothy 2:3	Our only hope for salvation

Name	Key Passage	Characteristics
God the Father	Galatians 1:1	First Person of the Trinity
God the LORD	1 Chronicles 13:6	Lord above all
God the One and Only	John 1:18	Unique, Divine One from heaven
God Who Sees (El Roi)	Genesis 16:13	Knows everything and cares
Great God	Daniel 2:45	Worthy of worship, majestic
Great King	Matthew 5:35	Absolute Ruler
Heavenly Father	Matthew 6:32	Eternal, loves His children, generous
Holy and Righteous One	Acts 3:14	Jesus, perfect in every way
Holy One	Proverbs 9:10	Pure, righteous Judge
Holy One of God	Mark 1:24	Absolutely pure One Who came from God
Holy One of Israel	2 Kings 19:22	Pure, divine head of the nation
Holy One of Jacob	Isaiah 29:23	Awesome, perfect leader of Israel
Holy Spirit	Titus 3:5	Righteous, present with us

Name	Key Passage	Characteristics
Holy Spirit of God	Ephesians 4:30	Seals, grieved with peoples' sin
Hope of Israel	Jeremiah 14:8	Savior of the nation, trustworthy
I AM (Jehovah)	Exodus 3:14	Eternal LORD
Immanuel	Matthew 1:23	God with us
Israel's Creator	Isaiah 43:15	Brought the nation into existence
Jealous	Exodus 34:14	Righteous zeal
Jesus	Matthew 1:21	Savior, Redeemer
Jesus Christ	Roman 3:22	Fully man, fully God
Jesus of Nazareth	John 18:5	Raised in Nazareth
Jesus Our Lord	2 Peter 1:2	God, worthy of our total allegiance
Judge	2 Timothy 4:8	Righteous, gives recompense
Judge of All the Earth	Genesis 18:25	Ruler, final authority
King	1 Timothy 1:17	Ruler over all, head of the eternal kingdom
King of Glory	Psalm 24:7	Awesome majesty

Name	Key Passage	Characteristics
King of Heaven	Daniel 4:37	Aramaic words for Supreme Ruler over all
King of Israel	John 1:49	Sovereign, Ruler of His people
King of Kings and Lord of Lords	Revelation 19:16	Above all rulers
King of the Ages	Revelation 15:3	Sovereign over all time
King of the Jews	John 19:19	Ruler of Israel
King of the Nations	Jeremiah 10:7	Sovereign of all governments and peoples
Lamb	Revelation 22:1	Sits on eternal throne, gave His life for us
Lamb of God	John 1:36	God's atoning sacrifice for our sins
Last Adam	1 Corinthians 15:45	Opposite of first Adam, who sinned
Lawgiver	James 4:12	Legislates, saves, destroys
Light of the World	John 8:12	Dispels darkness, gives life
Lion of the Tribe of Judah	Revelation 5:5	Leader, irresistible strength, majesty
Living God	Deuteronomy 5:26	Lord of life, alive, sovereign

Name	Key Passage	Characteristics
Living One	Revelation 1:18	Resurrected Lord, source of life
Lord (Adonai)	Isaiah 6:1	Master over all, owner of all, Ruler
LORD (Jehovah)*	Psalm 11:4	Eternal, sovereign
LORD Almighty (Jehovah-Sabaoth)	2 Samuel 6:2	All-powerful, awesome
Lord God (Adonai-Elohim)	Daniel 9:3	Omnipotent master
LORD God (Jehovah-Elohim)	Genesis 2:4	Majestic power, awesome
LORD God Almighty	Psalm 89:8	All-powerful, Sovereign Ruler
LORD Is My Banner (Jehovah-Nissi)	Exodus 17:15	Victorious, leads us in triumph
LORD Is Peace (Jehovah-Shalom)	Judges 6:24	Security, comfort
LORD Is There (Jehovah-Shammah)	Ezekiel 48:35	Present with His people
Lord Jesus Christ	1 Corinthians 1:7	Title of deity, resurrected and ascended
LORD Most High	Psalm 47:2	Greatness, exalted above all
Lord My God	Psalm 86:12	Deep, personal relationship with Adonai

* Translated as "LORD of Hosts" in the New American Standard Version.

Name	Key Passage	Characteristics
LORD My God	Ezra 9:5	Deep, personal relationship with Jehovah
Lord My Savior	Psalm 38:22	Divine Deliverer
Lord of All	Acts 10:36	Absolute Ruler
Lord of All the Earth	Joshua 3:13	Authority over all the world
Lord of Glory	1 Corinthians 2:8	Great splendor, perfection
Lord of Heaven	Daniel 5:23	Aramaic words for Sovereign Ruler
Lord of Kings	Daniel 2:47	Greatest sovereign
Lord of Lords	Deuteronomy 10:17	Greatest of all, Ruler of rulers
Lord of Peace	2 Thessalonians 3:16	Gives stability, security
Lord of the Earth	Revelation 11:4	Supreme Ruler
Lord of the Harvest	Luke 10:2	Rules efforts to bring people to heaven
Lord of the Sabbath	Matthew 12:8	Final authority over all life
Lord of the Whole World	Zechariah 6:5	Is in control of the universe
Lord Our God	Daniel 9:9	Adonai our Elohim, merciful, loving

Name	Key Passage	Characteristics
LORD Our God	Deuteronomy 6:20	Jehovah our Elohim, personal
LORD Our Maker (Jehovah-Hoseem)	Psalm 95:6	Powerful Creator
LORD Our Righteousness (Jehovah-Tsidkenu)	Jeremiah 23:6	Just, pure, holy
Lord, the LORD Almighty*	Isaiah 10:23	Punishes evil and arrogance
LORD Who Heals (Jehovah-Rophe)	Exodus 15:26	Delivers, compassionate, heals our infirmities
LORD Who Makes You Holy (Jehovah-M'Kaddesh)	Leviticus 20:8	Purifies, makes holy
LORD Will Provide (Jehovah-Jireh)	Genesis 22:14	Compassionate, meets our deepest needs
Majestic Glory	2 Peter 1:17	Awesome, radiant
Majesty in Heaven	Hebrews 1:3	Sovereign Ruler
Maker	Proverbs 14:31	Creator, Originator, Divine Architect
Maker of All Things	Jeremiah 10:16	Designer of everything, all-wise
Master	2 Timothy 2:21	Lord, leader
Messiah	John 1:41	Anointed One of God, prophet, priest, and king

* Translated as "Lord, God of Hosts" in the New American Standard Version.

Name	Key Passage	Characteristics
Mighty God	Isaiah 9:6	Ruler, above all the universe, all-powerful
Mighty One	Joshua 22:22	Greater power than anything in the universe
Mighty One of Israel	Isaiah 1:24	Powerful Sovereign of Israel
Mighty One of Jacob	Genesis 49:24	The powerful God Jacob served
Morning Star	Revelation 22:16	Brilliant, awesome
Most High	Daniel 4:17	Exalted above all other gods
Most High God	Daniel 4:2	No one greater, does miracles
Name	Leviticus 24:16	Personifies God, represents His divinity
Offspring of David	Revelation 22:16	Promised Messiah, descendant of David
One of Sinai	Judges 5:5	The LORD who gave the Law
Overseer	1 Peter 2:25	Leader, guardian
Portion of Jacob	Jeremiah 10:16	Spiritual possession of the nation

Name	Key Passage	Characteristics
Prince	Acts 5:31	Jesus, divine royalty on the throne
Prince of Peace	Isaiah 9:6	Brings peace to people and nations, source of security
Prince of Princes	Daniel 8:25	Highest and greatest of all
Prophet	John 7:40	God's spokesman
Redeemer	Job 19:25	Brings His people back to God, rescuer
Resurrection	John 11:25	Source of new life and immortality
Righteous One	Acts 7:52	Jesus, the innocent, pure One
Righteous Servant	Isaiah 53:11	Does right always, serves
Rock	Deuteronomy 32:4	Security, stable, faithful
Rock of Israel	2 Samuel 23:3	The nation's security, foundation
Root of David	Revelation 5:5	Descendant of King David

Name	Key Passage	Characteristics
Root of Jesse	Romans 15:12	Descendant of David's father
Ruler	1 Timothy 6:15	Sovereign, King, Judge
Savior	Luke 2:11	Saves from penalty of our sins
Savior of Israel	Isaiah 45:15	Deliverer of God's people
Savior of the World	1 John 4:14	Makes salvation available to all
Seed	Galatians 3:19	Descendant of Abraham, true Hebrew
Servant	Isaiah 42:1	God's faithful messenger (Messiah)
Shepherd	Hebrews 13:20	Compassionate leader
Shepherd of Israel	Psalm 80:1	Leads, enthroned
Son	Hebrews 1:8	Intimate relationship with God the Father, divine
Son of David	Matthew 21:9	Descendant of David
Son of God	Luke 1:35	Second Person of the Trinity
Son of Man	Mark 10:45	Stresses Christ's humanity

Name	Key Passage	Characteristics
Son of the Blessed One	Mark 14:61	Unique relationship with God
Son of the Most High	Luke 1:32	Worthy of worship
Son of the Most High God	Mark 5:7	Eternal relationship of deity
Sovereign	Jude 1:4	All-powerful, absolute authority to rule
Sovereign LORD (Adonai-Jehovah)	Jeremiah 32:17	Eternal Master, sovereign
Spirit	Romans 8:26	Intercedes, knows all
Spirit of Christ	Romans 8:9	Elevates Christ, indwells believers
Spirit of Glory	1 Peter 4:14	Guarantees our eternal bliss
Spirit of God	Genesis 1:2	Third Person in the Trinity
Spirit of Grace	Hebrews 10:29	Gives mercy and forgiveness
Spirit of His Son	Galatians 4:6	Causes us to know God intimately
Spirit of Holiness	Romans 1:4	Righteous, points people to Christ
Spirit of Jesus	Acts 16:7	Guides, communicates

Name	Key Passage	Characteristics
Spirit of Life	Romans 8:2	Gives life, gives freedom
Spirit of Sonship	Romans 8:15	Places us in God's family
Spirit of the Living God	2 Corinthians 3:3	Active in our hearts
Spirit of the LORD	Micah 3:8	Gives power, transforms
Spirit of the Sovereign LORD	Isaiah 61:1	Anoints, comes upon us
Spirit of Truth	John 16:13	Abides in us, proceeds from the Father
Spirit of Your Father	Matthew 10:20	Speaks through believers
Stone	1 Peter 2:4	Cornerstone, precious
Strength	Psalm 59:17	All-powerful, mighty
Sun of Righteousness	Malachi 4:2	Holy, heals
Truth	John 14:6	Accurate, reliable, trustworthy
"Unknown Name"	Revelation 19:12	Only Jesus knows this name
Vine	John 15:1	Source of life and goodness

Name	Key Passage	Characteristics
Witness	Revelation 3:14	Messenger of God
Wonderful Counselor	Isaiah 9:6	Helps believers deal with all situations
Word	John 1:1	Eternal God, communicates with us
Word of God	Revelation 19:13	Personification of God's message
Word of Life	1 John 1:1	God's messenger of hope for a dying people

[Note: The distinction between the Hebrew words LORD (Jehovah) and Lord (Adonai) is found only in the Old Testament. There is only one word in the the New Testament for "Lord" and it comes from the Greek word *kurios*.

Names in parentheses in the above table are the Hebrew titles.

The names that appear on this list and chart are from *The Holy Bible: New International Version*. Other translations may vary.]

Chart of God's Names

Name	Passage	Characteristics	Promises	Commands	Response
God of Glory	Psalm 29:1-11	LORD (Jehovah) Glorious (3, 9) Thunders (3) Powerful (4) Majestic (4) Awesome (5, 7, 8, 9) Eternal king (10)	Gives strength (11) Blesses with peace (11)	Recognize His majestic strength and glory (1,2)	Everything shouts "Glory!" (9)
Heavenly Father	Matthew 5:43-48	Gives good things to all (45) In Heaven (45) Perfect (48)		Love enemies (44) Pray for persecutors (44) Be like Father (48) Be perfect (48)	
	Matthew 6:5-15	Unseen (6) Sees (6) Knows our needs (8)	Rewards humble prayers (6) If we forgive, we'll be forgiven (14) If you don't forgive, we won't be forgiven (15)	Pray in private (6) Pray the way Christ instructs (9-13)	
	Matthew 6:25-26	Takes care of animals (26) Knows our value (26)	Will take care of you (26)	Have peaceful attitude (25)	
	Matthew 6:32-34	Knows our needs (32)	If we seek Him, all will be met (33)	Seek first His kingdom and righteousness (33) Don't be anxious (34)	

Note: Verse numbers are in parentheses.

Chart of God's Names

Name	Passage	Characteristics	Promises	Commands	Response

My Prayer Journal

(Make additional copies of this page if needed
for more prayer journal space)

Date	Prayer Request	God's Answer

My Prayer Journal

Date	Prayer Request	God's Answer

My Prayer Journal

Date	Prayer Request	God's Answer

My Prayer Journal

Date	Prayer Request	God's Answer

My Prayer Journal

Date	Prayer Request	God's Answer

How to Lead a Group
of People to Know God Better
by His Names

ﾟﾟ

This 31-Day Experiment (*Knowing God by His Names*) has been used by Bible study groups, men's groups, women's groups, families, groups preparing for a missions trip, new believers groups, Sunday school classes, and entire churches.

Doing this 31-Day Experiment together as a group has lots of benefits:

1. Everyone will be studying the same passages of Scripture during a month.

2. The whole group will be united together in learning to know and love God.

3. People will share their prayer requests with others in the group. Everyone will grow in his or her faith as members pray for one another and experience God's answering their prayers.

4. Individuals will see how the Lord is working in one another's lives.

5. Members can encourage one another in their relationships with the Lord and in sharing their faith in God with other people.

Here are some guidelines to start using *Knowing God by His Names* with your group:

1. Remind the people of the purpose of your group—and the need to deepen their relationships with the heavenly Father.

2. Introduce the 31-Day Experiment goal—to build a habit of spending 20 to 30 minutes each day with the Lord in Bible study, prayer, and application of God's Word to life.

3. Show how the book fits into the purpose for your group. Share ideas and passages of Scripture from the "Knowing and Loving the One True God" section, and motivate the people to seek to deepen their understanding of the character of God for the next month.

4. There are 31 days of study. Do the first day together as a group with the leader showing how to do the study. Encourage group members to all start on the same day (preferably the next day) so that each person will always be on the same experiment day. If at all possible, try to meet weekly. Therefore, when the next meeting occurs, they will have done six days of the experiment.

5. Plan to do the experiment with your group in five weeks. Each week the group members should start the experiment days on the day after the group meeting. On the day of a group meeting, members should not do the day's experiment. Rather, they can spend that day reviewing

their notes for the previous six days and thanking the Savior for all He has done in their lives.

6. When the group settles on the day they all want to start the experiment, send an e-mail reminder of the date to each person as well as a reminder of the date, time, and place for each weekly meeting. Designate one e-mail address to which people can send e-mails about the things they are learning, prayer requests, and answers to their prayers. Send all the e-mails received to the whole group each day to encourage people to keep doing the experiment. This will help build group unity and spiritual growth.

7. Encourage members to use a Bible dictionary, Bible concordance, or word-study book when they need to understand passages better.

8. Encourage the group to bring their Bibles and their *Knowing God by His Names* books to each weekly meeting (which should last from one to one and a half hours).

9. When you meet, discuss each day of the previous week's experiment consecutively. Ask people to share with the group what they learned and how it has affected their lives.

10. If your group is large, you may want to divide into smaller subgroups, preferably five to six people in each group. Ask the people in the group or smaller subgroups to call one another during the week to see how each person is doing, answer any questions, and pray together on the phone. In this way, each person will receive several phone calls a week.

11. At the conclusion of each group meeting, pray together, praising the triune God for all He has done and asking Him for consistency to do the experiment faithfully each day. Pray that each person will look forward to meeting with the Holy One daily and will experience His presence in their lives during the week.

12. Use the following as a simple format for the weekly meetings.

Weekly Group
Participation Outline

Subject: Knowing God by His Names

Content: Review the previous six days

Tips for the Leader

1. Prepare your lesson early, asking the Holy Spirit to give you ideas on what to teach and how to draw all the people into the discussion. Be creative. Use a variety of ways to communicate, such as videos, music, drama and objects—whatever it might take to make the lessons meaningful.

2. Start with an icebreaker as a way of getting to know one another a little better.

3. Begin with the whole group together, interacting on what they learned that week. Or if your group is large, you may want to split up into the subgroups. This will allow a greater number of people to share about their experiences.

4. Find out what hindrances they encountered as they sought to meet with God each day. Discuss how to discipline yourselves to consistently spend time with the Lord in the midst of hectic schedules.

5. Let everyone give input on the first day's topic before going on to the second day's topic.

Questions for Discussion

1. How did your meeting with Jehovah go each day this past week?

2. What did you have to do to set aside the 30 minutes each day?

3. What did you learn about walking with the Son of God? Loving God the Father? Obeying the Spirit of Truth?

4. What answers to prayer did you receive? What are you still praying about?

5. What kinds of responses did you receive when you reached out to other people?

Closing

1. Celebrate all that the Chief Shepherd has done during the past week.

2. Discuss the week ahead and the passages you will be studying. Build interest and excitement for the new things you will encounter and learn.

3. Close in group prayer. Lead in praising the Messiah for His working and in asking Him to draw everyone closer to Himself during the week.

4. Motivate the people to pray earnestly for one another during the week. Remind them to phone others and send e-mails about their experiences. Encourage each person to share their faith with people who don't know the Prince of Peace personally.

At the end of the five weeks of the experiment:

1. Conclude with a special dinner, or order pizza. Build a fun atmosphere.

2. Make the time a celebration of completing the experiment.

3. Focus attention on the Lord and how wonderful He is.

4. Share testimonies of changed lives and healed relationships.

5. Introduce another 31-Day Experiment. Plan for what you will do next to keep growing in faith and building your group fellowship.

6. Motivate the members to invite their friends to participate in the new experiment. Encourage them to pray for their friends that they might join the group and get involved in knowing God by His names.

7. Encourage each person to start their own "Knowing God by His Name" group with their friends and neighbors.

Additional 31-Day Experiments

Now that you have developed a habit of meeting with God each day, I hope you will want to continue to spend time alone with the risen Lord. He is the Vine from whom you can receive daily life and nourishment. Intimacy with Him continues and increases as you daily open your mind and heart to the heavenly Father.

The 31-Day Experiment series has been designed to assist you to daily devote time to enhance your relationship with God. Whether you are a new Christian or have been one for a long time, these 31-Day Experiments will help you establish an intimate relationship with God. You will experience for yourself the joy of discovering God's truth from the Bible.

All the experiment books are designed like the one you have just completed. Each book focuses on a different theme in the Bible and includes relevant passages for you to study.

At the end of each experiment you'll find a number of simple Bible study methods or ideas for further growth. These will help you investigate, on your own, more of the truth that the Holy Spirit wants to teach you.

These books are designed to help you get into God's Word and get God's Word into you.

Growing Closer to God

This 31-Day Experiment book will help you increase your knowledge of God by having you look at passages in which you can discover more about His ways and perspectives. The process of continuing to know God intimately will affect every area of your life and actually will begin to transform you into the kind of person He wants you to be. Some topics in the book are:

- God's Plan to Provide for My Needs
- Assurance of Eternal Life
- Peace with God
- Experiencing the Power of God
- Living with New Purpose
- Passionately Loving God
- Guidance from God
- Living by the Spirit
- The Pleasure of Pleasing God
- Triumphing over Trials and Temptations

Three additional Bible study methods are also explained. The first is "One-a-Day Bible Topics." You will learn how to find out all that God says on any biblical subject that interests you. The second is "One-a-Day Scripture Meditations" that will show you how to get the most from focusing on a passage of Scripture.

The third is "Big Lessons from Little People," in which you will investigate the lives of biblical people. To start you off, 15 people are suggested. Each one can be studied in 30 to 45 minutes. The Holy Spirit can teach you some vital lessons through these ordinary individuals.

Discovering God's Unique Purposes for Your Life

Do you ever wonder why God made you like you are? What is your purpose for being alive? What do you think about yourself? Regardless of who you are or what you do, this experiment book will help you put your life in sharper perspective and give you insight into the person God wants you to be.

Are you maximizing your spiritual gifts? Are you using your time wisely? Are you making the most out of your life? Are you pleasing God, the One Who made you unique for a unique purpose?

You will study these questions and find biblical answers as you work through the book. You will spend several days studying passages in which God says significant things about how to look at yourself. Your confidence will come from understanding who you are in God's eyes. Then for the rest of the days you will study passages that, if followed, will help you live life to the fullest. You will learn practical things you can do to make your life count for Christ.

This fascinating experiment will give you biblical answers so you can overcome personal doubts and weaknesses. Clearly and powerfully, it will help you see the real truth about yourself from God's point of view. You will receive specific suggestions for living your life to the fullest with significance. Your relationship with the Lord will be enhanced as you spend time daily with Him and discover what the Bible says about how to understand your uniqueness.

Here are some topics you will study to help you develop a biblical self-image:

- What does God say about you?
- Learn to invest your life wisely

- How to improve yourself
- Discover and develop your spiritual gifts
- Getting God's blessings into your life
- Learn to be truly happy
- What does it mean to "renew your mind"?
- Love like God loves
- Rejoice in difficulties
- Maximizing your uniqueness
- Live with your ultimate future in mind

These and other important topics will help you develop a positive perspective on yourself and your life.

About the Author
Dick Purnell

Dick Purnell is an internationally known speaker and author. He has spoken in all fifty states in the United States as well as in twelve other countries. He is the Executive Director of Single Life Resources, a division of Campus Crusade for Christ. Dick and his wife, Paula, are on the national speakers' team for FamilyLife Marriage Conferences.

He has authored thirteen books, including his latest, *Finding a Lasting Love*. Some of his other books are: *Becoming a Friend and Lover, Free to Love Again, Building a Strong Family, Making a Good Marriage Even Better, Discovering God's Unique Purposes for You* and *Growing Closer to God*.

A graduate of Wheaton College, Dick holds a master of divinity degree from Trinity International University, as well as a master's in education, specializing in counseling, from Indiana University. He is an adjunct professor at New Life Bible College in Moscow, Russia.

Dick has been featured on many national television shows, including *The Coral Ridge Hour*, *The 700 Club,* and *The Nashville Hour*. He has been the main guest on many radio programs, such as *FamilyLife Today*, *Moody Broadcasting*, *Truths That Transform,* and *America's Family Counselors*.

Bring Dick Purnell to Your Area

Dick Purnell speaks to audiences throughout the United States, Canada, and in many other countries. For information about the wide variety of topics he presents, contact him at:

Dick Purnell
P.O. Box 1166 • Cary, NC 27512 • USA
Phone (919) 363-8000
Web site: www.DickPurnell.com

Other Excellent Harvest House Books
by Dick Purnell

Finding a Lasting Love

Singles make up 40 percent of the American adult population, and most of them want to find their lifelong mate. Dick Purnell, Executive Director of Single Life Resources, reveals the questions, answers, and insights on dating he shares through conferences, interviews, and articles. Going straight to the heart of the matter, he discusses:

- insights for understanding the opposite sex
- how to avoid short-circuiting a good relationship
- suggestions for finding a potential partner and
- what God's Word says about relationships

Finding a Lasting Love is beyond a "how to" for the dating reader. It's a biblical exploration of relationships and an invitation to approach dating and life with a healthy, growing faith.

Other 31-Day Experiment Bible Studies

Growing Closer to God

Discovering God's Unique Purpose for You